BETRAYAL IN RELATIONSHIP

Some Causes Of Betrayal And How To Tackle Them

CLAIRE PATTERSON

INTRODUCTION

Some types of betrayal are as painful as having one's heart mercilessly ripped out of their chest. Everyone who has been betrayed in a relationship can agree that betrayals aren't good for a person. When it comes to comprehending what betrayal truly entails, it is critical to recognize that it can take many forms.

In a relationship, how you define betrayal may differ from how another person defines it. So, before we get into the various ways it can occur in a relationship, let's clarify what betrayal in a relationship is.

This is due to the fact that different people have different values. In general, betrayal in a relationship occurs when a presumptive contract, trust, or confidence is broken.

Acts of betrayal destroy your trust in your partner, and depending on the type of betrayal, some people may have trust issues for the rest of their lives.

Finding out about a partner's infidelity can be painful since it affects so many facets of who you are. It might make the one who has been betrayed question their own attractiveness or ability to judge others, as well as the world's inherent goodness.

This is so because our relationships are based on the flimsy understanding that the people we worry about most will behave mostly in the same manner they always have. A betrayal can destroy that trust and provide room for doubt about what is happening in one's private, little world.

This book aims to expose various types of betrayal to you as well as the true reasons for them.

The goal is not to fill you with negative emotions, but to arm you with winning strategies for overcoming a betrayal from a loved one and moving on to finding true love once more.

By the end of this book, you will have gained the courage to embark on a new chapter in your life, even if you have previously been betrayed by a partner.

CHAPTER ONE

Some Types Of Betrayal In Relationship

Sexual infidelity, conditional commitment, a nonsexual affair, lying, establishing a coalition against the partner, absence or coldness, losing interest in sexual relations, contempt, injustice, selfishness, and breaking vows are a few examples of betrayal in romantic relationships. Typically, betrayal in a romantic relationship happens when there is a breach of a putative contract, trust, or confidence, which causes moral/psychological difficulty.

Types of betrayal

No act of betrayal is minor and should be treated as such. These types of betrayal, on the other hand, cut deep, like a warm knife slicing through butter.

1. Intangible acts of betrayal

Wait a second. When we hear the word "infidelity," our minds automatically conjure up the notion that one partner in a relationship must be having sex with someone else in order to be considered an unfaithful partner.

What if this isn't completely accurate? Are there any other scenarios that, while not sexual, qualify as acts of infidelity?

Yes is a simple and conventional answer. Infidelity is defined by Wikipedia as a violation of a couple's emotional and/or physical exclusivity, which typically results in feelings of anger, sexual jealousy, hurt, or rivalry.

Another peculiar aspect of this definition is the selection of synonyms for infidelity, one of which is straying. This definition, along with the highlighted synonym, implies that not all types of infidelity are physical/sexual.

Non-sexual forms of betrayal in relationships can be just as damaging as sexual forms of betrayal. Here are a few examples of non-sexual forms of betrayal in relationships.

- Financial infidelity is a type of infidelity in which financial obligations are involved. While it is convenient to have your own funds as an independent adult, some financial betrayals can be a major annoyance to your relationship if your partner finds out. For example, being in debt or engaging in unhealthy financial habits such as gambling.
- Emotional acts of cheating occur when you begin to develop a deep emotional attachment to someone other than your partner, particularly if that emotional involvement replaces the emotional connection you should have with your partner.

2. Selfish acts of desperation

Every now and then, you must remind yourself that you are a human being worthy of love and attention.

This will help you prioritize your physical and mental health because being in a romantic relationship forces you to focus on your partner, sometimes at the expense of your own.

While taking care of oneself is necessary at times, desperate acts of selfishness are examples of betrayal that hurt just as much as cheating on a partner.

Constantly acting in excessively self-indulgent ways without regard for your partner's needs and desires will strain your relationship over time. The unfortunate thing about this type of betrayal is that you may not feel the heat in your relationship right away.

If your partner is patient and can tolerate many of your excesses (or if you are the one who is this way in the relationship), they may be able to delay showing you how they feel about your actions.

However, doing so for an extended period of time can be detrimental to your relationship. According to research, only taking and receiving (selfishness) can have a negative impact on a relationship. They can lead to feelings of inferiority, loneliness, and social isolation.

3. Failure to defend your partner, particularly in public

Have you ever been in a situation where people make fun of you for no apparent reason, and instead of standing up for you, your partner tends to make awkward gestures and laughs along with the 'jokes?'

Depending on the people and circumstances, it can be just as painful as outright cheating.

The thing about relationships is this. You agreed to more than just having casual sex with your partner when you agreed to date, marry, or be in a relationship with them. You agreed to be their partner/teammate. This implies that you should advocate for them whenever possible.

Allowing them to take the heat in public while standing on the sidelines will only harm your relationship. It may only be a matter of time before they call you out on it.

Because it is excruciatingly painful!

4. Lying

Lying to your partner or spouse may have a greater impact on them than betrayal of others. Lying is usually done in response to a perceived wrong action.

When you have committed an action that you believe is wrong and would prefer to keep it hidden from your partner, it is possible that you will resort to the obvious solution, which is to lie to them.

The most painful aspect of this type of betrayal is that your partner will often keep a large portion of their life away from you. When a lie is exposed, it frequently triggers a flood of negative emotions in the minds of the other person in the relationship.

Lying has a far greater impact on your partner than simply avoiding an immediate confrontation.

Lying can cause your partner to second-guess themselves and wonder what else you're hiding from them.

Furthermore, depending on what you've been lying to them about, this second-guessing may cause your partner to begin doubting everything you tell them. As a result, trust has been shattered and feelings of insecurity have arisen, which may take some time to heal.

5. Making use of your partner's past against them

This type of betrayal hurts more than you can imagine. It implies that you are unworthy of being trusted with your partner's past, and it may also indicate that you are emotionally immature.

One of the many reasons your partner confided in you was most likely to seek your support and assistance during a difficult time. They may have made a mistake in the past that they will have to deal with for the rest of their lives, even if it is only emotionally/mentally.

Part of your job as a sign of your commitment to them is to help them overcome their past mistakes and hurt, not to use them as verbal jabs when you argue with them.

Using your partner's past against them is a deep betrayal, and you may find them physically recoiling from you when you do this to them.

6. Refusing to acknowledge your partner's sexual desires

The sexual aspect is an important aspect of most intimate relationships. Relationship betrayal does not only occur when one partner cheats on the other. A conscious rejection of physical intimacy with your partner, especially for no apparent reason, can have far-reaching consequences for your partner's emotional and mental health.

If you continue to make advances toward your partner and they continue to reject you, you may be tempted to believe that you don't appear physically attractive to them or that they simply don't like you that much. If this concept is not clarified, it can lead to depression or self-doubt.

7. Emotional apathy/coldness

Being available to your partner entails more than just being physically present. It also implies that you should be physically and emotionally present with them.

Another form of betrayal that, while intangible, hurts is emotional coldness and detachment. Consider having a partner who lives in the same house as you but cannot be reached in times of emotional distress. If this emotional detachment persists for an extended period of time, it can strain the relationship.

8. Disregard

Your partner can and should be a variety of things to you. One of them is not a slave. When you start acting in ways that make your partner feel inferior to you or that you are more important than they are, your relationship begins to deteriorate.

These acts of disrespect can be subtle at times. They could be pronounced at other times. Disrespect for your partner, in any case, is a dangerous form of betrayal. If you believe your partner is being disrespectful to you, watch this video to learn how to deal with it.

CHAPTER TWO

Causes Of The Betrayal

If you've ever experienced any of these types of betrayal, you'd agree that they're painful and can leave you wondering why you've been left to deal with such betrayal in your relationship.

In any case, here are some possible explanations for the betrayal in your relationship.

1. Previous negative experiences

If your partner has had traumatic experiences in previous relationships, they may express betrayal toward you. They may show you disrespect or attempt to be emotionally detached from you (to prevent heartbreaks again).

2. A sense of isolation and despair

If you are lonely and emotionally estranged from your partner, you may seek solace elsewhere. This can sometimes result in unprecedented acts of betrayal in the relationship.

When we think of betrayal in a relationship, we usually imagine it in a dramatic, almost cinematic setting—an affair, a one-night stand in the middle of a fight, or even walking out in the middle of the night. But the truth is that many betrayals are far more subtle—and they are rarely glamorous. Sure, there's the betrayal when you cross paths with the also the more mundane, day-to-day betrayal that occurs when you emotionally distance yourself from your relationship and your partner over time.

Also, if you have unmet emotional needs or a desire for love whiles your partner is emotionally/physically unavailable; you may be in a difficult situation.

And it's critical to understand all of these different types of betrayals because even the most seemingly innocuous forms can slowly erode your relationship. Here are some things to keep an eye out for.

Non-Physical Infidelity

In a relationship, not all infidelity is physical. There are many behaviors that easily pass the test for infidelity without involving any touching at all—in fact, infidelity does not have to involve sexual attraction or even another person.

Financial infidelity is a major form of betrayal that is rarely discussed. While some financial independence is healthy—and you shouldn't feel obligated to tell your partner every time you buy yourself a t-shirt or a cup of coffee—more secretive financial behavior can be extremely concerning. It's a breach of trust, especially if those secrets involve debts or spending that affects your partner's financial security or credit.

Emotional cheating is another type of non-physical infidelity that resembles more traditional infidelity. Developing an emotional dependency on another person, particularly when it replaces your emotional connection with your partner, can be as damaging as cheating. But, on the other hand, having friends is healthy—and sometimes distinguishing between innocent friendships and emotional infidelity can be difficult.

If you're attracted to the person, fantasize about having an affair with them, or notice that the connection is negatively impacting your relationship; you'll know you're dealing with an emotional affair rather than a harmless friendship.

Betrayal in Other Forms

Other types of betrayal may not rise to the level of infidelity, but they can still wreck havoc on your relationship. Some are deliberate, while others you may not even realize you're doing. However, you must be aware of when you are disrespectful to your partner, as these small betrayals have the potential to erode your relationship over time. One of these methods is to reveal personal information about your partner—specifically, information that they would not want others to know. This is a difficult balance to strike because, on one hand, you have every right to talk to your friends, vent, and seek advice. But if it's something so deep and personal to your partner that you know they'd never want anyone else to know, keep it close to your chest.

One of the most difficult positions you may be placed in is managing your relationship with your partner's friends and family—this is an area where you may end up clipping into betrayal without malice, but because you feel trapped. . For example, if you are aware that your partner has a difficult relationship with their mother, but their mother tries to win you over, shares information about them, or drags you into a conversation in which they want you to divulge personal information; you may have to work hard to respect your partner's boundaries.

People you're attracted to or flirting with are another important group to be aware of. Sharing private information about your partner or sharing secrets in general can be dangerous, especially if you're attracted to or know your partner dislikes the person. In fact, it is frequently the beginning of an emotional affair.

Betraying Any Agreements You've Made

While some betrayals are universal, every relationship is filled with individual agreements you've made to each other. Some may be explicit, while others may be tacit, but there are boundless agreements and understandings in a partnership. So, if you agreed to take more time off work but then refuse to do so, you have betrayed your trust. It's also a betrayal of the emotional foundations on which a relationship is built to take advantage of your partner, be critical of them, and become complacent. So be aware of how your relationship has always appeared, what unspoken dynamics you've established, and ensure that you're meeting those expectations.

CHAPTER THREE

Betrayal Significance In Relationships

It is impossible to have a flawless marriage. It's alright. However, it may be an indication that your partner will cheat if they constantly let you down, utter white lies, hide their feelings, and other such little betrayals. That's because honesty and trust are fundamental to creating a strong connection.

If your partner has bad habits or a personality that justifies their bad behavior, there may be more significant issues. The best indicator of future conduct is, after all, past behavior. According to Bustle, the founder of Double Trust dating and a dating guru is Jonathan Bennett. Therefore, it's not a tremendous leap to imagine your partner might be unfaithful if they have a history of lying, deceiving, and manipulating others.

You must speak up as soon as you become aware of even the smallest betrayals. Bennett suggests that the best course of action is to talk to your partner about bothersome behaviors rather than tolerating them merely because they seem insignificant. Cheating is an example of a little pattern of poor behavior that might eventually escalate to a greater betrayal. Here are a few instances of little betrayals that, according to experts, might escalate into more serious issues if left unattended.

1. Financial deception

If you learn that your partner is not being honest about their spending patterns, especially if you have a joint bank account, it may be a sign that there is no loyalty or trust in the relationship. And later on, this can result in other problems. This does not imply that talking about money is simple. It isn't, not even for the healthiest of relationships. Even so, there is such a thing as financial infidelity, and it might be the beginning of a trend.

According to Bennett, this "occurs when one partner [keeps] the other in the dark regarding financial matters." "This may involve hiding money, making unauthorized purchases, or engaging in any kind of financial deceit or manipulation. It suggests a pattern of dishonesty."

2. Retaining contact with former lovers

As long as they are upfront and honest about it, it is not a betrayal if your spouse keeps in touch with their ex. However, if they're doing it to keep this person in their "back pocket," perhaps to date them again in the future, it could be an indication they're not interested in the relationship."Many people keep ex-partners or friends on their "back burner" relationships "just in case."

Having fallback options, on the other hand, can create easy opportunities to cheat, especially if the relationship hits a rough patch." So, if you're unhappy with your partner's friendships, talk about it. Why do they want to keep in touch with their ex? What type of relationship is this? By conversing you might get to the bottom of whatever they're looking for in terms of connection.

3. Telling a Lot of White Lies

Everyone tells a white lie now and then. That's fine. However, if your partner makes it a habit, it may be an early warning sign that they will not be trustworthy in the future.

Joshua Klapow, PhD, clinical psychologist and host of The Kurre and Klapow Show, states that a person who doesn't seem disturbed by lying—even little lies to avoid issues or disagreements in the relationship—may be more prone to cheat. "That's because they can handle a lot larger betrayal of infidelity if they can lie more easily," the author explains.

4. Asking Others for Emotional Support

Couples should be able to communicate with their friends and family outside of their romantic partnership. But confiding in a few close pals is not the same as engaging in a "emotional affair."

"If your spouse forms a deep emotional bond to someone else but keeps it a secret from you, it's quite likely that Later on, it will result in true cheating," warns Bennett. Oftentimes, people get into these kinds of relationships to avoid having uncomfortable conversations with their partners. It's "frequently challenging" when a relationship isn't working out nicely. According to psychologist Tina B. Tessina, PhD, and author of the fourth edition of her book, How to Be a Couple and Still Be Free, "transfer affection to someone else rather than incurring the emotional risk of talking to a spouse about unhappiness."

However, emotional affairs can be avoided by having honest and open dialogues. According to Dr. Tessina, most relationship issues may be resolved quickly if both couples are open to discussing them.

5. Easily becoming envious

Being a little envious in a relationship is very acceptable. However, if your partner acts envious all the time, it can be a sign that they are preparing a liaison.

"Jealousy often leads to worry, which may also be a warning that your spouse is more inclined to cheat," "If your partner gets angry and jealous easily, it may indicate that they are more prone to cheat."

6. Online Flirting

While online chatting with friends is plainly permissible, it can be a dangerous sign of betrayal if your partner starts to flirt with other people behind your back." . "It's a problem if they're flirting with someone on [social media] or a dating app with the justification that they're simply conversing and not meeting," she asserts. Dating expert and CEO of Cyber-Dating Expert Julie Spira tells Bustle that it might be an emotional betrayal that invites something more serious. So, if it bothered you, bring it up as soon as you can.

7. Keeping Their Phone Safe

In a strong, lasting relationship, you shouldn't have anything to conceal. It is acceptable to have some privacy and a social life apart from the partnership, but this should not entail lying or keeping things a secret.

It may be an indication of infidelity if your partner has started to become extremely protective of their phone. "If your partner starts putting up additional barriers and passwords around their phone and computer, this could be a sign that they are more prone to cheat," says the author.

8. Refusing Emotional Support

If your partner does not offer you emotional support while you are struggling, it may be an indication that they are not emotionally committed to the relationship."A partner who cannot/won't join you in your times of misery is more likely to cheat," says Dr. Klapow. When you need them the most emotionally, they are not there to listen to your problems, provide you physical comfort, comfort you, or know what to do when you are angry.

9. Being Too Concerned With Oneself

To keep a relationship healthy, it's important to preserve your own selves, have your own friends and interests, and take pleasure in some personal space. However, if your partner consistently puts themselves first, it's not a good indicator for the future of your relationship.

According to Dr. Klapow, they prioritize taking care of themselves over others when making insignificant life decisions that have little to no impact on you. They may be more inclined to cheat if they do not have the "we" mentality and instead focus on themselves, thus "maybe it's where they want to eat supper, changing the temperature in the house to suit their requirements, or the music in the car."

10. Being Difficult to Contact

A person who is emotionally and physically available in a relationship is one who is "all in." So be on the lookout if your lover disappears and seems unconcerned with how you feel.

According to therapist Kimberly Hershenson, LMSW, if your partner is often hard to contact and doesn't respond to calls, messages, or emails despite the fact that you know they are accessible, they may be more likely to cheat.

Don't fail to notice it. It's imperative to voice your feelings over their actions, according to Hershenson. "Describe what you require and offer suggestions for improvements. It could be time to find someone else if they are unable to match your needs."

11. Investigating Others

Although it's normal to pay attention to other people, it's not a good sign for your relationship if your partner is continually glancing over their shoulder at everyone who passes by.

Hershenson contends that your partner is more likely to cheat later if you catch them making sexual advances toward other individuals. Of course, there is no certainty in this, but it is crucial to be aware of these small warning signs.

According to Dr. Klapow, "These behaviors and traits characterize a person who is more inclined to avoid confrontation in the relationship, is not emotionally attached with you, has less empathy, and prioritizes their own needs." While this does not imply that they will cheat, it does suggest that if there is tension in the relationship or if they feel attracted to someone outside of it, they will be more inclined to go the "easy option," which is to satisfy their wants. Even while not all cheating is preventable, you can talk to your partner about your worries and attempt to come to an understanding before an affair happens.

CHAPTER FOUR

Steps To Get Over Betrayal

If you have experienced any of the sorts of betrayal mentioned, you might need to put a lot of work and devotion into healing.

You can get past romantic betrayal and build an admirable life for yourself, no matter how much grief and hurt you experience.

This study explores the ways in which betrayal can be dealt with in relationships and whether commitment might encourage reconciliation.

Everyone's road to healing is different, thus there are no set rules for how to recover from a betrayal in a relationship. However, by taking the following 15 actions, you may overcome a romantic betrayal.

1. Recognize the betrayal

Someone you trusted has deceived you, shattering your heart to pieces. Although it is tragic, you find it hard to believe. You can't fathom why or how your partner would treat you in this way. You therefore turn to denial. Regardless of whether the betrayer did it on purpose or not, your trust has been broken. The first step to getting well and over it is realizing it.

2. Recognize your feelings

How do you feel about the betrayal? Angry? Shocked? Sad? Disgusted? Ashamed? You can experience a flurry of emotions.

Name them instead of rejecting or repressing them. Hurt feelings shouldn't be covered up with denial. When seeking to recover from betrayal in a relationship, it is crucial.

3. Don't hold it against yourself.

Your sense of self-worth declines when someone betrays you. It's normal to blame yourself for your partner's misdeeds.

When you repeat the betrayal in your head, you could think that if you were taking care of your partner's physical and emotional needs, they wouldn't have resorted to another person.

But treachery is always a decision. Because of a terrible relationship, no one is given carte blanche to do anything they want.

4. Take some time apart

It would be ideal if you could take some time to reflect on what has happened. No matter how fervently your lover attempts to get in touch with you and beg for forgiveness, don't give in.

Let them know you need some time to yourself to process and think rationally. It doesn't mean that you've made up your mind to part ways with them. You can analyze the betrayal and get clarity by taking a break.

Marriages that have been betrayed find it challenging to recover. You're unsure if you should end the connection or try to mend the harm.

Taking a break is crucial for your emotional and mental wellness, regardless of what you choose.

5. Be saddened by the loss of trust.

Because losing a loved one is a loss, people express their sorrow when they learn of their passing. Being deceived is a violation of trust, and it is only reasonable to feel hurt.

When dealing with a betrayal in a relationship, be ready to experience all five stages of grief: denial, anger, bargaining, sadness, and acceptance. Not everybody reads them all. They might not even appear in this order.

However, so that you can deal with the loss in a healthy way, let yourself grieve in your own way.

6. Resist the urge to retaliate.

The adage "an eye for an eye makes the whole world blind" is undoubtedly one you've heard. Your partner betrayed your confidence, and you must be furious with them. It's only normal to desire to hurt and torture the person who betrayed you. Retaliation is not one of the many constructive strategies to move past betrayal in a relationship, despite the fact that there are many others. It won't accomplish anything but slow down your recuperation. No matter how enraged you are, don't betray the one who betrayed you.

7. Tell someone you trust everything.

You could feel as though you can't trust anyone after being tricked by someone you care about. However, asking for emotional support from close friends and family members is a crucial step in the healing process. If you feel uncomfortable, you are not obligated to reveal the gory specifics of your partner's betrayal. Simply state how the occurrence makes you feel. Converse with someone who can maintain objectivity and give you their brutally honest opinion rather than adding more fuel to the fire. No reliable confidantes close by? You may always consult a relationship specialist on how to move past betrayal in a relationship.

8. Create a strategy for dealing with betrayal.

It's time to create a strategy for dealing with betrayal now that you've had some time to reflect on what happened. Yes, you remain incensed, alarmed, and grieved. You're finding it difficult to handle betrayal.

But if you keep dwelling on how they've harmed you or revisiting that upsetting memories in your thoughts, you won't be able to recover. Now is the time to decide how to move forward. Do you want to repair your relationship and make things right with your partner?

Do you want to call it quits on your relationship for good or just temporarily? Do you want to start journaling and practicing meditation? Do you intend to seek a therapist's help in order to mend your broken heart? Analyze it.

9. Think about it.

Once you've regained control of your emotions, it's a good idea to spend some time reflecting. If you want to offer your spouse an opportunity to atone for their actions, think about your relationship, how it was before the betrayal, and what needs to change.

It's common to think that you could have handled the situation differently and that your spouse wouldn't have wounded you as deeply when dealing with betrayal and asking "how to get over a betrayal in a relationship." Even while we should all do better, your partner's betrayal is a result of their choice and has nothing to do with your character or actions.

If your relationship had issues before to the betrayal, you both must cooperate to resolve them if you want to maintain it. However, your partner must first own up to their mistakes and express sincere regret.

10. Discuss the matter with your partner.

It could be awkward for you to confront the individual who deceived you. However, it's imperative to speak with your spouse and let them know how their actions have affected you for your own peace of mind.

If they've been pleading with you to listen to them, you can give them the opportunity to share their side of the story. Note whether they make an effort to defend their behavior or show sincere remorse. Use "I" statements, maintain your composure, and speak politely.

11. Try to be able to forgive.

To forgive is not to overlook, tolerate, or justify the injustice that has been done to you. Even if you choose not to, you are under no obligation to make amends with that person.

You should only think about giving your relationship another shot if the other person shows signs of sincere remorse. Please accept their apologies even if they are not guilty. Even if they do not, you must forgive the person and let go in order to fully move on from a betrayal.

12. Remove the plug

Was this your partner's first time betraying your trust? Do they comprehend how much suffering they have brought on? Have they expressed regret and taken ownership of their actions? Are they habitual violators, or was this a mistake that happened just once? End the relationship if this is not the first time they have betrayed your trust. If you continue to be in a relationship with someone who repeatedly betrays your trust and causes you harm, there is no reason for them to stop.

13. Be willing to place a new trust.

You don't have to believe everything someone says. Take a baby step at first and small, controlled risks. Instead of blindly trusting your lover, if you've decided to give them another opportunity, do so gradually.

14. Regain your trust in yourself.

When dealing with betrayal, one of the most important steps to take is to trust yourself. To trust others, you must first trust your ability to make sound judgments and slightly adjust your trust indicator.

15. Look after yourself.

You've been through a lot, and now it's time to put yourself first. Moving on does not take place overnight. However, whether you decide to end or rebuild the relationship, you must begin with small steps to practice self-care and regain your confidence.

16. Terminate contact with your ex.

Heartbreak hurts so badly because of science: According to Elle Huerta, creator of Mend, an app and online community aimed at assisting people post-breakup, you truly experience withdrawal-like symptoms following a breakup since the feel-good hormones you acquired from your spouse are suddenly gone.

She continues, "You start to want those feel-good chemicals when your lover is no longer there." "You'll struggle to move forward and possibly become stuck months or even years later if you give in to this feeling and visit your ex again." Starting by severing all ties is beneficial. It enables you to let go of your attachment to your ex. She says that there isn't a set guideline on getting in touch with your ex. Communication that is brief and infrequent, such as

"Hey, may we converse for a minute? I'm struggling with this"—could be OK. Just be careful they don't turn into routine "innocent check-ins." Your objective is to break these energetic ties, not to keep forging new ones, because every time you speak to someone, you open up another energy bond between you.

17. Keep in mind the negative.

Idealizing the ex-partner is a common reaction following a breakup. And even though you don't want to downplay your relationship's positive aspects, you also don't want to become fixated on them.

Make a note of all the drawbacks of your ex-partner or relationship and regularly review it to find a happy medium. This mental activity helps balance out all the obsessive thoughts about what you miss about your ex and why they were so great—even if they weren't.

This thought keeps coming even if your ex was great or not.

CHAPTER FIVE

Easy But Effective Way To Overcome Betrayal

Have you ever been betrayed by someone you care about, or even a friend? I know I have, and just because you've been betrayed don't necessarily mean you've been cheated on. You are aware that betrayal occurs when trust between two people is broken, and you are aware that this may result in some sort of moral conflict. You can tell the difference between a romantic relationship that fails and leaves you both feeling that promises have been broken and a disagreement between friends.

You may feel as if you've been betrayed, or it may simply mean that one person feels abandoned by another. My point here is that emotional betrayal is one of the most painful experiences anyone can have in life, so in this book, I'll give you eight effective strategies for emotional healing. To begin, emotional trauma can leave deep emotional scars that trigger in the same areas of the brain that physical pain does. Betrayal can occur as a single event or as a series of events. It can also be caused, intentionally or unintentionally. It is frequently unexpected, and it can leave a person feeling powerless and unable to protect themselves from the pain it causes.

At first, you may feel outrage, denial, and disbelief. However, the experience can feel surreal, almost like an out-of-body experience. It can now quickly become an emotional rollercoaster, with extremes ranging from intense anger and rage to deep depression and sadness. Not only is the individual attempting to process the event, but they are also grieving the loss of what was and what could have been. Physical manifestations include exhaustion, insomnia, nightmares, tense muscles, nausea, loss of appetite, and pain. However, when we reach a fork in the road, we can choose to act in ways that favor or hinder personal growth. We can either stay in a bad situation indefinitely or we can put it behind us for good. When we decide on a path, we remove all attachments; sometimes taking a step back is difficult, but it's necessary. Moving past the initial shock and dealing with the devastating pain that you experience when betrayed is also beneficial.

So you want to take a deep breath and mentally step back from the situation you're in. Try to detach yourself from all the emotions and perhaps imagine yourself as an unbiased reporter of the event, rather than the victim of the betrayal. So you want to identify what happened simply but factually, without any emotional explanation. So you want to learn all of the facts without passing judgment on what happened, and you want to take a mental snapshot of this emotional space so that you can refer to it later to try to gain some insight. When you are in situations where your emotions are running high, use the neutralizer as you go through this experience. So in the movie Men in Black, starring Will Smith and Tommy Lee Jones, they have this device called a neutralizer that they use on people to make them forget certain events,So with that in mind, I want you to erase the imprints of betrayal. The betrayal may be so deeply embedded in our subconscious minds that it is difficult to remove. Meditation or hypnosis can assist in reaching the source of previous deception and accelerate the healing process. I recommend quietly meditating for a few minutes each day with the goal of digging into the contents of your brain and erasing old memories or thought patterns that keep you stuck. Being honest about how the betrayal made you feel Recognize and accept that you may have several feelings about the betrayal that compete with one another, and that's okay. Because these are your feelings, you want to own them and acknowledge them. However, be careful not to get caught up in a thought pattern involving a feeling or emotion that exaggerates your sense of self.

You may be feeling more or less hurt than you actually are. So, take the time to develop an emotional scale for how you feel today; this will help you track your emotional healing progress over time. Just remember that time is on your side, and everyone's timeframe is different. My ex-husband and I split up, and even though we decided to go our separate ways, it took years for us to heal from that experience. Just because you can't see the scars doesn't mean they aren't there. You don't have to accept this betrayal as your own. Don't, I repeat, don't beat yourself up; you're not to blame, and it's not your fault. As a result, we are each responsible for our own actions; no one can force you to behave in a certain way. As a result, life is a game of choices. Even if the betrayer tries to shift the blame, we all have choices. We all have things we can work on within ourselves, but that doesn't make you responsible for this situation; you're not to blame because you didn't cause it, so don't play the blame game. You know, whether or not to blame yourself or the betrayer, you will be trapped in a never-ending cycle of guilt with no way out. March by disposing of an object that represents your darkest moments in life. By doing so, you are consciously and subconsciously removing these terrible memories from your mind. Take ownership of your part in it. However, taking ownership of your part is not the same as taking ownership of the betrayal as a whole.

Again, this is not to say that you are to blame for the betrayal. You understand that the betrayer made the decision to take a specific action, and you are not to blame for that. You must move forward in order to regain a sense of safety and security. You must recognize the actions or mistakes that led to the creation of an opening; these are the areas where you must heal and apply new strategies moving forward. Do you, for example, need to learn to set and stick to clear boundaries? Do you struggle to express your emotions and beliefs clearly? Do you blindly give unearned trust? Do you tend to disregard red flags in order to avoid conflict? Do you fear being alone, so you compromise by maintaining a healthy relationship rather than not having one? Do you lack self-esteem or confidence, or are you easily manipulated by others? This is the process of determining your blind spots or areas to improve in order to avoid repeating the same patterns in future relationships or interactions. Being aware puts you in control and is the first step toward positive change. Trust yourself first, because the first person you must trust is yourself, so you should begin by developing a deep, unbreakable bond with yourself and your amazing abilities. Thus, know yourself and always affirm it. Make new promises to yourself each week or month, and keep those you know. Take small steps every day until it becomes a habit. There's no reason to put up with people who are dishonest. If you believe someone is untrustworthy, simply tell them you don't need them in your life.

For your own well-being, you must be picky about who you let into your life. Keeping people who do not inspire trust will only make you distrustful of everyone. It's critical to remember that the story we tell ourselves is what holds us hostage, not the person we're attempting to forgive. Forgiveness enables you to let go of your emotional baggage and move on. First and foremost, make the decision to forgive. So I've told you that betrayal has affected me, and you know how it leaves a deep wound that has impacted me in some way, but forgiveness is a time-consuming process. It doesn't happen overnight, so once you've set your Integers to forgive, a successful strategy is to mentally or verbally recite a mantra or affirmation of forgiveness on a daily basis or over a period of weeks, months, or years.

In the middle of heartbreak, it's crucial to look for oneself. Throughout the day, check in with yourself and ask: What do I need? A hot bath, a healthy salad, or a call to a friend could all be the cure.

Also be aware that low self-esteem and feelings of rejection can cause harmful behaviors like bingeing or purging and substance misuse, which can set off a depressed cycle. Exercise, good nutrition, and adequate rest will reduce how miserable you feel, he continues.

"Don't compare the length of your relationship with the length of your healing." Even "nearly romances" have the potential to be devastating.

Recognize that there will probably be voids left in your life after the breakup. "Let's assume you and your ex went to the movies every Friday." Now that you have a free Friday night, call your buddies and make plans instead of spending it by yourself.

Consider that while you were dating, you reduced your weekend habit of going hiking because your ex didn't share your love of the outdoors. Give yourself a chance to rekindle that passion and discover new activities now that you're single. If we're attempting to recover, we have to take measures to heal because "the universe meets us at the moment of action."

CHAPTER SIX

CONCLUSION

Some acts of betrayal, while not cheating or infidelity, cause as much pain as cheating or infidelity. In this book, we've discussed various types of infidelity and how they can devastate your relationship.

Take note of them, avoid them, and use the strategies discussed in the final section of this book to help you overcome past betrayals in your relationships.

www.ingramcontent.com/pod-product-compliance
Lightning Source LLC
LaVergne TN
LVHW020535160826
845677LV00015B/4072

* 9 7 9 8 8 4 6 2 9 0 6 5 5 *